T0392237

It's a Self-Esteem Revolution

How you see yourself is everything

Martine A. DeCambre

WESTBOW
PRESS*
A DIVISION OF THOMAS NELSON
& ZONDERVAN

WestBow Press books may be ordered through booksellers or by contacting:

WestBow Press
A Division of Thomas Nelson & Zondervan
1663 Liberty Drive
Bloomington, IN 47403
www.westbowpress.com
844-714-3454

Because of the dynamic nature of the Internet, any web addresses or links contained in this book may have changed since publication and may no longer be valid. The views expressed in this work are solely those of the author and do not necessarily reflect the views of the publisher, and the publisher hereby disclaims any responsibility for them.

Scripture quotations marked NKJV are taken from the New King James Version. Copyright © 1982 by Thomas Nelson, Inc. Used by permission. All rights reserved.

Any people depicted in stock imagery provided by Getty Images are models, and such images are being used for illustrative purposes only. Certain stock imagery © Getty Images.

ISBN: 979-8-3850-2256-4 (sc)
ISBN: 979-8-3850-2255-7 (e)

Library of Congress Control Number: 2024906329

Print information available on the last page.

WestBow Press rev. date: 10/07/2024

"He who walks in another's tracks leaves no footprints"
- Joan Brannon

Contents

Dedication

This book is dedicated to every child and every grown up child who needs to know how amazingly wonderful they are.

Excerpt from Desiderata
Max Ehrmann ©1927

"You are a child of [God]
No less than the trees and the stars;
You have a right to be here."

"Preserving your identity is life's most precious goal"
-Bruce B. Wilmer

Introduction

What is it about you that you just can't stand? The thing you won't tell anyone, or the thing that when mentioned by someone sends you into a tail spin? Do you spend days and nights wishing you were someone else, or just wishing and hoping and dreaming that just for once, you can just feel okay, really okay in your very own skin?

Wonder no more! We want to spend some time with you breaking this thing down called self-esteem. It's not a bad word, nor is it an elusive thing that you just can't seem to get a handle on, nor is it only for the lucky and the fortunate.

Let's take this "monster", simplify it and have you walk away feeling as though a breath of fresh air was blown your way.

Grab your favorite blanky, sit in your coziest chair, or go to your favorite place. Whatever you do, have a pen handy and put aside all beliefs you have right now about what you think self-esteem is and let's unpack this thing together.

"Courage is Commitment"
-Martine DeCambre

Chapter 1

WHAT IS SELF-ESTEEM?

The simplest definition of the term self-esteem boils down to this... *how you think or feel about yourself.*

Here are some terms that can be used instead of self-esteem...

1. Self Image
2. Self Confidence
3. Self Perception
4. Self Love

The bottom line is this, when you are alone and the loudest voices in your life are all quiet...
HOW DO YOU FEEL ABOUT YOU?

Low Self-Esteem

Describes someone who feels bad or ashamed of themselves; their quirks, their idiosyncrasies, their differences, their strengths, or their weaknesses. They are destroyed by other people's opinions about them and may take days, weeks, months, years

1

or NEVER to get over what someone has done to them, or said to them or said about them.

High Self-Esteem

Describes someone who feels good about themselves; their quirks, their idiosyncrasies, their differences, their strengths and even their weaknesses. You saying something bad about them is not going to cause them to run and hide or feel deep shame. They may think for a minute or two about your opinion and adjust their behavior or thoughts IF they feel they need to, BUT they will not be crippled or slowed down by it.

"A man can stand a lot as long as he can stand himself"
-Axel Munthe

Chapter 2

WHO ARE YOU?

Do you ever wake up in the morning or stop in the middle of the day and wonder "Who am I?" "How do I fit in this big ole world, or in my little world?"

You are not alone! If you have not asked this question of yourself, not even once, then you are not alive. This is a legitimate question we all have, or have had at one time or another.

I too had that question and from time to time still do, though not as often as I once did.

I decided that since God made me I would seek to get my answer from Him. Working on my Bachelor's of Science degree in Biology, I found myself sitting in class one day, and I made the quality decision that no matter what my philosophy, psychology or genetics professors had to say about God and why we are here, I NOT ONLY BELIEVED GOD.... I BELIEVED IN HIM, and have chosen to allow *Him* to define me and why I am here.

You see, this was how I figured it....all these PhD, tenured professors didn't seem so sure about what they were saying regarding who we are and why we are here. Everything was a conjecture, kinda up in the air, a theory of sorts....so I figured; let me see what God had to say about me. After all, He made me.

So I opened my Bible (my owner's manual) and this is what I found and this is just a sampling.

1. Psalm 139 :13 For You formed my inward parts;
   You [f]covered me in my mother's womb.
   14 I will praise You, for [g]I am fearfully *and* wonderfully made;
   Marvelous are Your works,
   And *that* my soul knows very well.
   15 My [h]frame was not hidden from You,
   When I was made in secret,
   And skillfully wrought in the lowest parts of the earth.
   16 Your eyes saw my substance, being yet unformed.
   And in Your book they all were written,
   The days fashioned for me,
   When *as yet there were* none of them.

This told me that God thought carefully about me before I even got here, so He must have some sort of important plan for me separate and apart from my parents.

2. John 3:16 For God so loved the world that He gave His only begotten Son, that whoever believes in Him should not perish but have everlasting life.

This told me that I was VERY LOVED.

3. Jeremiah 29:11 For I know the thoughts that I think toward you, says the LORD, thoughts of peace and not of evil, to give you a future and a hope.

This told me I have a very bright future.

4. Genesis 1:26 Then God said, "Let Us make man in Our image, according to Our likeness; let them have dominion over the fish of the sea, over the birds of the air, and over the cattle, over [a]all the earth and over every creeping thing that creeps on the earth."

This told me I was very important to God.

5. Ephesians 3:20 Now to Him who is able to do exceedingly abundantly above all that we ask or think, according to the power that works in us,

This told me that God was The Source of all I would ever need or want.

Please consider meditating on these scriptures until they really become a part of you. If you have children, begin teaching your kids how to read the Bible and show them how to let it become a part of their lives.

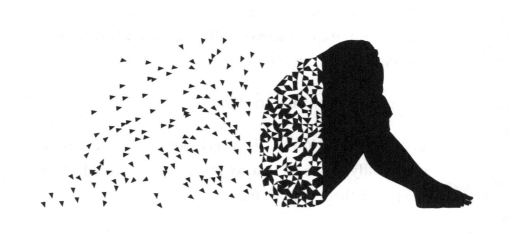

Chapter 3

HOW IS SELF-ESTEEM DESTROYED?

The question of how your self-esteem is destroyed suggests that your self-esteem can be built and strengthened. But let's tackle the difficult questions first.

Are we who other people say we are? Are we who we say we are? What if other people's opinion of us is really terrible? What if our opinion of ourselves is also not good? What then?

These types of questions are the ones that can be very confusing and makes time spent learning about and building your self-esteem well worth it.

So what are some of the possible ways your self-esteem can be destroyed?

Studies have shown that the building of one's self-esteem begins very early in life, but one can also be affected by circumstances that occur later in life. Please add to my list if you can think of any other reasons.

1. By parents who are not aware of how to build the self-esteem of their children.

2. By siblings who are not taught to be loving, kind and respectful towards each other

3. By other family members or acquaintances who are allowed to have access to your life and are not made aware of how to treat you with care.

4. By popular culture especially in the form of the news, social media, entertainers, athletes and etc. If these sources are allowed to take precedence in your life they will become your teachers and the result is often not good whatsoever. These strangers should **_NEVER_** have a front row seat in your life.

5. By peer pressure – this is a big one and no matter how old you are, you can fall victim to this. Parents please step up in your kids' lives and set the standard for them. Use this *Self-Esteem Handbook* and learn to be the LEADER in your own lives. Do not blindly follow others who have no clue about their life much more yours.

6. By abuse – oh boy this is a hot topic today. Abuse comes in many different forms and fashion. Verbal, physical, sexual, emotional, financial or spiritual abuse are all very serious types of abuse. Abuse is an epidemic today. In my opinion a very simple definition of the word abuse

is the ***Abnormal Use of.*** No one is to abnormally use you. Parents should not, boyfriends or girlfriends should not, friends should not, husbands or wives definitely should not. The best safeguard against abuse is a healthy self-esteem and moms and dads it starts with you. If you do not know enough about this topic – really use this *Handbook* and make it a part of your lives and your children's lives. A good, healthy self-esteem is so extremely necessary today. No one gets a free pass. A healthy self-esteem is like oxygen for our souls!!!!

7. By failures or mistakes. When you try to do something and it doesn't work out, one of the biggest temptations is to see yourself as a failure. What you call failure, I call an education. Listen, none of us are perfect, YET so many of us have become crippled today because of mistakes we have made. GET OVER IT! YOU HAVE TO! The only perfect person who walked this earth was Jesus Christ. He loves you and all He expects from you is obedience. A daily effort to admit when you are wrong and change; and to ask for His help when it's just a bit too much to do on your own. Never you ever let anyone hold your mistakes or failures against you. GET UP and MOVE ON!!!! The only failure that is final is if you refuse to get up and try again.

8. By hurtful words. There are people today living under a bridge, completely given up on life because of what

someone said to them or even what someone didn't say. Words are very powerful <u>especially</u> in the lives of children. If you have been the recipient of someone's hurtful words spoken over you or the lack of kind words spoken to you, then this *Handbook* is especially for you because one of the best lessons you are ever going to learn is that of being responsible for you. You are ultimately responsible for how you feel. Parents you are ultimately responsible for your children's emotional health. Do everything you can to help them as much as you possibly can. Being a parent is a huge responsibility and one that should not be taken lightly.

"No matter who or what made you what you have become, that doesn't release you from the responsibility of [allowing God to make you] over into what you ought to be."
-Ashley Montagu

"Our lives improve only when we take chances – and the first and most difficult risk we can take is to be honest with ourselves"
-Walter Anderson

Chapter 4

HOW IS SELF-ESTEEM BUILT?

Here comes the fun part!

A healthy self-esteem is not a mystery. Not some elusive thing that only the lucky seem to have. BUT!!! and this is a big but …. It can be very fragile and is one of the most important parts of yourself you must take the time to find out about, nurture and never ever trade for a handout.

It is never to be taken lightly, nor is it for sale. It forms the fabric of who we are, yet is so fragile that it must be nurtured every single day, like an infant, until it is strong enough to stand on its own, and even then, must never ever be taken for granted.

Abusers know that if they can erode your self-esteem they own you. They will damage your self-esteem with such subtlety, that before you know it; they have inserted themselves in your lives committing more serious harm than you could ever imagine. People have lost their lives because they have allowed an untrustworthy person access to their lives in ways <u>THEY NEVER SHOULD HAVE</u>.

Here are some really neat and easy ways to build and secure your self esteem. Please feel free to add to this list....

1. ***<u>Learn to trust yourself.</u>*** You know that feeling, that still small voice that says something doesn't feel, sound or look right? ***<u>Pay attention</u>*** and be ready to make any necessary changes to keep yourself safe. Keep your head on a swivel. Do not fall asleep. This is your life.

2. ***<u>Get to know yourself.</u>*** We have a wonderful exercise at the end of this book. Take the time to know you. What makes you happy, sad, angry or frustrated? Pay attention. Feelings are faithful reporters. Let no one tell you otherwise. Feelings are important. Though they should not rule our lives, we must pay attention to them. This is what makes journaling so very helpful.

3. ***<u>Gain a good reputation with yourself.</u>*** The best way to do this is to write down or save your wins. Have a Brag Box just for you. If you win a competition and get a certificate, copy it and place it in your Brag Box. If you created something, take a picture and place it there. If someone gave you a beautiful card, save it in your Brag Box. If someone said something nice to you write it down and place it there. The goal of this is to save your wins and look at them often. This world can be a

bit rough and everyone seems to have an opinion lately – especially on social media. You must know who you are, or these insensitive people can destroy you. Don't let them! Your Brag Box is your permission to feel good about you!

4. ***Surround yourself with positive, life-affirming people***. If I could get on a loud speaker and have this heard around the world I would. People who will make you smile, be kind to you, have your back and not talk about you behind your back and are going somewhere in life are not easily found. It is said that you should look in your phone at the people you talk to the most and in 5 years you will become more and more like these people. If this scares you, it's time to seriously assess who you call friends and begin little by little to distance your self from the following people: complainers, whiners, abusers, gossipers, backstabbers, those engaged in illegal activities and those who are just heading nowhere in life. It may seem lonely at first, but just remember this is YOUR life. You only have one and at some point you have to decide to make the best of it.

5. And last but certainly not least...***Get to know God.*** Spend time with Him. Read your Bible. This has changed my life. I say this as often as I can....<u>one of the most important things you can ever do in your life, is to get to know the Voice of God.</u> Contrary to some

people's opinion, He still speaks to us and in us. To this very day…I always have a current journal, and I take the time to sit with God and listen. I figured He gave me 2 ears and 1 mouth so prayer has to be just as much about listening as it is speaking. As a matter of fact, it has become for me more listening than speaking. Allow God to love you and tell you who you are to Him. His love is enormous. You can never out love Him nor out give Him. His love will 'wreck' you (in a good way) and you will never be the same again. He will teach you HOW to love yourself. He wants you to love yourself. Not in a narcissistic way, but in a way that enables us to love others. He is a Good, Good Father. The one who sticks closer than a brother or a sister, and the One who sticks around when everyone decides it's not in their best interest to stay.

Here are a few Bible verses for you (NKJV of the Holy Bible)

1. **Jeremiah 1:5**

   "Before I formed you in the womb I knew you"

   Contrary to popular thought, you were not first thought of by your parents. No…God your Maker is the one who first thought about you and allowed you to come through your parents and gave you to them to raise in the love and knowledge of Him.

2. **Psalm 139:14**

   "I am fearfully and wonderfully made. Marvelous are your works"

   You are made in the Image and Likeness of a Powerful and Loving God. Never you ever forget that. You are worth more than rubies, diamonds or gold. I don't care who you are or what you have done. Get to know Him.

3. **John 3:16**

   "For God so loved the world that He gave His Only Begotten Son [Jesus] that whoever believes in Him shall not perish but have everlasting life."

   God loved you and I so much, that He sent His One and Only Son from Heaven to come to earth to teach us a better way and to be the ultimate buy back for us. He is worth learning about. You will never regret it because He is the Ultimate Self-Esteem Builder ☺

These Bible verses are taken from the NKJV of the Holy Bible and references the God of Abraham, Isaac and Jacob and His Son Jesus Christ.

"No one can make you feel inferior without your consent"
-Eleanor Roosevelt

Chapter 5

BENEFITS OF A STRONG SELF-ESTEEM

1. You are much happier
2. You are more confident
3. You trust yourself more
4. You are more willing to try new things
5. You are more willing to go after your dreams
6. You build healthier and mutually satisfying relationships
7. It becomes more difficult for anyone to abuse or misuse you
8. You take better care of yourself
9. You resist the urge to give up
10. You just feel better about yourself ☺

Please feel free to add to this list……

"When our center is strong, everything else is secondary"
-Elie Wiesel

Worksheet 1

IMPORTANT WORDS!

"Sticks and stones may break my bones but words will never hurt me"
- Believed to be written by Alexander William Kinglake in 1844

"Words cut deeper than knives. A knife can be pulled out, words are embedded into our souls"
-William Chapman

Which of these quotations ring more true to you?

In my opinion the second one does. Words are extremely powerful, and I have reached the point in my life where I am extremely careful about what I allow to come out of my mouth, what I listen to and what I allow to be spoken around me or to me.

If I do not want to see it or experience it in my life **_I DO NOT SAY IT_**!!

Now that we got that out of the way, let's make a list of some really powerful words you can begin to say that can change your entire life.

Just say them. At first you may not believe them, but keep saying them, they will eventually take root. Kinda like planting a seed. Put it in the ground, water it, give it a little love, sunshine and time and before you know it a little shoot will show up and then a magnificent tree. Don't keep digging up the seed. Just let it sit and do its thing ☺

"Self-esteem is the reputation we acquire with ourselves."
- Nathaniel Branden

ASSIGNMENT

1. Please add your own Important Words to make 30 in all, or more!

2. Feel free to copy this list and make a habit of speaking these Important Words over yourself daily until they become a part of you.

POWER WORDS

1. I AM LOVABLE
2. I AM BEAUTIFUL / HANDSOME
3. I AM SMART
4. I AM UNSTOPPABLE
5. I AM STRONG
6. I AM LOVING
7. I AM MADE IN GOD'S IMAGE AND LIKENESS, AND HE LOVES ME
8. I AM UNSHAKEABLE
9. I AM INTELLIGENT
10. I AM BEAUTIFUL INSIDE AND OUT
11. I AM CAPABLE
12. I AM COURAGEOUS
13. I AM PERFECT JUST THE WAY I AM
14. I AM CONFIDENT
15. WHATEVER I SET MY MIND OR MY HANDS TO I EXCEL AT
16. I AM RESPECTFUL

17. I AM WORTHY OF RESPECT
18. I AM WORTH IT
19. I AM GOOD ENOUGH
20. SOMEONE SOMEWHERE APPRECIATES ME AND THE THINGS I DO
21. NO! YOU ARE NOT THE ONLY ONE WHO WILL OR CAN EVER LOVE ME (this is a red flag for abusive people. One of their favorite lines is "I am the only one who will love you or who will put up with you", or some version thereof.)
22. I AM BELIEVABLE
23. I HAVE INTEGRITY
24. I MAY BE ALONE BUT I AM NOT LONELY
25. I LOVE ME
26. _____
27. _____
28. _____
29. _____
30. _____

"The way you treat yourself sets the standard for others"
- Sonya Friedman

Worksheet 2

WHO DO YOU THINK YOU ARE?

How do you see yourself? What opinion do you hold of yourself?

1. Are you a good person?
2. Are you a bad person?
3. Are you worth someone else's time?
4. Are you someone only one person or no one could ever love or put up with?
5. Is your life worth living?
6. What is it about you that makes you smile?
7. What is it about you that irks your soul?
8. What do you have to look forward to?
9. Has life hurt you soooo bad that you think you will NEVER recover or lift your head again?

These are questions or variations of them WE ALL MUST ANSWER. And trust me; the answers to these questions do not come overnight. But stay tuned.

When you first do this exercise, it may be a bit tough, but I strongly believe that if you make this *Self-Esteem Handbook* a consistent part of your life, a daily guide, so to speak, this will become easier and easier; and as time passes the list will become longer and longer….the only way to find out is to try it for yourself!!

ASSIGNMENT

1. Write down 10 things you like about yourself. You may only be able to do 5 at first, but keep trying; you will get to 10 before you know it.

2. Add to this list as you discover more amazing things about you.

3. Save this list in your Brag Box and refer to it often ☺

I'll go first….. I am a great cook!   ☺

1. _____
2. _____
3. _____
4. _____
5. _____
6. _____
7. _____
8. _____
9. _____
10. _____

"Make a true estimate of your own ability
and then raise it 10 percent"
-Norman Vincent Peale

Worksheet 3

BE THANKFUL!

ASSIGNMENT

1. Get yourself a little journal, or print some ruled paper from the internet and staple them together or print several copies of the next page and staple together.
2. First thing every morning when you wake up, before you do anything else, take 5 minutes and write down 5 things you are grateful for.
3. If you are having a hard time thinking of things you can be grateful for start with the alphabet.

For Example

"I am soooo thankful that…."

A – I have AIR to breathe
B – I can BREATHE
C – I have a CAR to drive

Whatever is your reality, you can be thankful….just find something, anything, to be thankful for – it will change your life!

My Thankful Daily Journal

Today's Date: _____/_____/_____

S   M   T   W   R   F   S

"TODAY I am so thankful for" ………

1. _____

2. _____

3. _____

4. _____

5. _____

"Gratitude is the well-spring of Life. Practice
it and you will benefit from it"
- Martine DeCambre

The Conclusion of the Matter

It is my hope that this little journey you took with me will forever change your mind and your life.

Your self-esteem, how you see yourself, is extremely important. It can make or break you. So many people today are walking around with a very damaged sense of who they really are and it plays a huge factor in the decisions they make and the long term success of their lives.

The work that you do...any work that you do in developing an independent sense of who you are, rooted in what God has to say about you is WORTH IT.

You will be able to pass this on to your children and your children's children and put an end to generations of damage.

God loves you and has BIG plans for you. I do not care how bad things may look now. Keep on keeping on...this work pays dividends for years to come.

Never you ever forget that you are PRICELESS; A MASTERPIECE of enormous value. Put your hands in the

Hands of your Maker and go do *your thing* that God has set aside for you to do. Ask Him what that is, He will show you.

Psalm 16 NKJV
King David

² *O my soul*, you have said to the Lord, "You *are* my Lord, My goodness is nothing apart from You."
⁵ O LORD, *You are* the portion of my inheritance and my cup; You [b]maintain my lot.
6 The lines have fallen to me in pleasant *places*; Yes, I have a good inheritance.

Get to know God The Father. It's our life's most precious goal. He IS our Self-Image because we were made in HIS Image and in HIS Likeness. Get to know Him and you will get to know you.

Read The Holy Bible in a version you can understand. This is your owner's manual. In the same way that you would read the owner's manual for a car you bought in order that you may know exactly how it functions…read the Bible to learn about you.

God made us. He knows exactly how we function, and He left an owner's manual for us to follow and it's called The Holy Bible.

This, my dear friend, is the true "secret" to a healthy self-esteem and therefore "The Conclusion of This Matter".

I will share one of my most favorite poems with you. Hopefully it will become one of yours as well because it is so true ☺

"It's a Self Esteem Revolution!"
- Martine A. DeCambre

♥   ♥   ♥   ♥   ♥   ♥   ♥   ♥   ♥   ♥

A RETURN TO LOVE

"Our deepest fear is not that we are inadequate. Our deepest fear is that we are powerful beyond measure. It is our light, not our darkness that most frightens us. We ask ourselves, 'Who am I to be brilliant, gorgeous, talented, fabulous?' Actually, who are you not to be? You are a child of God. Your playing small does not serve the world. There is nothing enlightened about shrinking so that other people won't feel insecure around you. We are all meant to shine, as children do. We were born to make manifest the glory of God that is within us. It's not just in some of us; it's in everyone. And as we let our own light shine, we unconsciously give other people permission to do the same. As we are liberated from our own fear, our presence automatically liberates others."
Marianne Williamson, A Return to Love: Reflections on the Principles of "A Course in Miracles"
Quoted in that amazing movie, COACH CARTER.

Printed in the United States
by Baker & Taylor Publisher Services